I0415280

Betrayal

The Democratic Party's Destruction of America's Cities

John Perazzo

World Studies Books
Thornwood, New York
Email: wsbooks25@gmail.com

Copyright © 2019 by John Perazzo

All Rights Reserved. No part of this book may be reproduced in any manner without written permission from the author, except in the case of brief quotations included in critical articles and reviews.

Published in the United States

In honor of the monumentally important work that is being done by courageous American heroes like Brandon Straka, Charlie Kirk, and Candace Owens

The Democratic Party Myth

Among the most widely accepted claims in American political discourse today is the notion that the Democratic Party, regardless of whatever flaws it may have, is the party that stands up for the well-being of the so-called "common man." We are told that Democrats in public office advocate for a wide range of policies designed to improve the lives of the poorest and most powerless among us. The task of this pamphlet is to scrutinize these claims by examining, specifically, how the policies implemented by political leaders in Democrat-run cities across the United States have affected the economic conditions and crime rates in those places.

Regarding economic matters, the official Democratic Party Platform explicitly pledges to:

- create "an economy that grows incomes for working people, creates good-paying jobs, and puts a middle-class life within reach for more Americans";
- "develop a national strategy ... to combat poverty," with particular "focus on ... underserved communities"; and
- implement "a comprehensive agenda to invest in America's cities" and to "support entrepreneurship and small business growth" therein.[1]

With regard to crime, this same Democratic Party Platform articulates a belief that the existing American criminal-justice system is highly inequitable and thus must undergo transformational "reform." "Instead of investing in more jails," the Platform explains, we need to:

- end the "mass incarceration" that allegedly "targets individuals solely on the basis of race, religion, ethnicity, or national origin";
- "invest more in jobs and education" than in "jails and incarceration";
- "reform mandatory minimum sentences";
- "close private prisons and detention centers"; and

- "abolish the death penalty, which has proven to be a cruel and unusual form of punishment" that "has no place in the United States of America."[2]

The Democratic Party presents these promises and policy prescriptions as though they were fresh and novel ideas capable of changing American society for the better. But mountains of empirical evidence lead us to a very different conclusion. In city after city where Democrats have been in charge politically for an extended period of time, we find exceedingly high—indeed, often colossal—levels of poverty and crime. And the longer those Democrats have been in charge, the worse the conditions tend to be. In short, Democrats have transformed a host of once-great metropolises into urban prisons where the common man—particularly the black and Hispanic common man on whose behalf Democrats typically claim to speak—has been grievously harmed by one destructive Democratic policy after another.

But that is only half of the story, for the relationship between political leaders and their constituents is a two-way street. People in public office would have no political power whatsoever, had they not been elected by a majority of their constituents. If the voters residing in any particular city remain unfailingly loyal to Democrats despite the fact that Democratic policies have repeatedly proven to be ineffective or even destructive, then those voters are wholly complicit in creating whatever economic or social afflictions may plague them. They are willing and active partners in an aimless political tango.

Compounding this tragedy is the simple fact that things did not have to turn out this way. The Democrat-run cities that have declined so badly in recent decades were not always undesirable places in which to live. Many of them were once prosperous, thriving centers of industry and culture. And while some of those cities were governed during their better days by Republicans, others were governed by Democrats. *However, it is vital to understand that those were Democrats whose mindset bore virtually no resemblance to that of the radical Democrats who became increasingly influential and numerous from the 1960s onward.*

The Democratic Party's Radicalization

Up until the Sixties, the Democratic Party was a liberal party in the sense that it clearly viewed government intervention—as opposed to free-market principles—as the best remedy for all types of societal problems. But by no means was it a hard-left, countercultural party that despised capitalism, disparaged American traditions, detested the nation's founders, or viewed the United States as a force for evil, rather than good, on the world stage.

Consider, for example, the policies and attitudes espoused by President John F. Kennedy in the early 1960s. As the popular author and broadcaster Larry Elder has pointed out, Kennedy rejected the use of racial preferences and quotas to regulate hiring and promotion decisions in the business world, calling instead for "mak[ing] sure we are giving everyone a fair chance"; in short, he argued for the proverbial "level playing field." In 1962 the president said that "tax rates are too high" and should be cut immediately, so as to enable the nation to "achieve [a] more prosperous, expanding economy." A lifetime member of the National Rifle Association, Kennedy believed that the Second Amendment unambiguously guaranteed an individual right for Americans to bear arms. And with regard to foreign relations, the president emphasized the need for an America whose unrivaled power and unwavering sense of purpose would "let every nation know … that we shall pay any price, bear any burden, meet any hardship, support any friend, oppose any foe to assure the survival and the success of liberty."[3]

But even as JFK was promoting his vision of a strong America founded upon principles like limited government, individual rights (as opposed to group rights), low taxes, fiscal responsibility, a strong national defense, and a sense of national pride, the early roots of the Democratic Party's radical transformation were beginning to take hold in our cultural soil. Emblematic of this development was the rise of the openly defiant, raging, revolutionary movement known as the New Left, which was personified by such figures as Bill Ayers, Bernardine

Dohrn, and Tom Hayden, and by groups like the Students for a Democratic Society and Weatherman.

By the end of the decade, the New Left, with its incessant combativeness and its open contempt for traditional values, had alienated most Americans and was a dying phenomenon. But its adherents were determined to keep their radical objectives alive by any means necessary, so they altered their tactics. Specifically, they resolved to carve out a new home for themselves *within the Democratic Party*. They resolved to infiltrate and then radicalize that party by means of a "New Politics" movement that would purge it of all its classical centrist liberals—i.e., those Democrats who had vigorously defended American exceptionalism and opposed Communist totalitarianism in decades past.[4] This radical takeover of the Democratic Party was fully achieved by 1972, as evidenced by the nomination of George McGovern as a presidential candidate whose antiwar platform cast America's military involvement in Southeast Asia as an immoral, imperialistic abomination and called for a swift and complete U.S. withdrawal. Additional key elements of McGovern's platform included massive cuts in military spending and large tax increases for high earners.[5]

From that point forward, the radicals who were now in charge of the Democratic Party aimed to work within the so-called "system" in a manner which they had previously regarded as "selling out." The most effective way to transform society, they now reasoned, would be to quietly infiltrate America's major institutions—the schools, the media, the churches, the entertainment industry, the labor unions, *and of course a major political party*—and to then impose their agendas gradually and incrementally from those avenues of power. Central to this endeavor was the effort to push the Democratic Party and its agendas ever further to the political left. It was *these* newly radicalized Democrats and their ideological descendants—*not* the Democrats of the pre-1960s era—who were, and who continue to be, chiefly responsible for the degradation of their party and of so many American cities that they control politically.

The eminent author and conservative activist David Horowitz writes that "the leftward slide of the Democratic Party began with the [1972] McGovern campaign, when the anti-Vietnam left marched into its ranks and assumed positions of power in its congressional party."[6]

In a similar vein, historian Ronald Radosh explains that it was between 1968 and 1972 "that the Democratic Party began its leftward shift" toward the extreme radicalism that is its unmistakable hallmark today. He elaborates:

> "[T]he old Democratic Party ceased to exist. The Left, which at first boycotted working with the Democratic Party, moved *en masse* into its ranks. They essentially took it over.... Not only did the party adopt the mantle of the antiwar movement, [but] the social programs it advocated identified the party with the rise of crime, the influence of drugs, the decline in moral standards, and the breakup of the traditional family structure.... [A]fter 1968, the Democrats stood in the public's eye for a new kind of liberalism, one that spelled permissiveness and moral nihilism....
>
> "With the 1972 [presidential] campaign, and the eventual leadership of the Democratic Party falling into the hands of George McGovern, the triumph of the New Politics group was apparent.... As McGovern fought a bitter battle for the nomination with his arch-rival, Senator Henry 'Scoop' Jackson of Washington, the two poles of the Democratic Party were starkly revealed for the first time. The defeat of Scoop Jackson showed that the Center had eroded, and that the social and economic policies of the party's left wing were now the accepted doctrine of the Democratic leadership."[7]

Because, as one *Investor's Business Daily* editorial puts it, "the Democratic Party has been drifting more or less continually to the left" ever since 1972,[8] the sentiments that President Kennedy articulated in the early Sixties would be resolutely rejected by the Party today. Indeed, JFK himself would find no home in the Democratic Party as it is currently constituted. Neither would traditional liberals like Daniel Patrick Moynihan or Scoop Jackson.

Author and publisher Peter Collier explains how the Democratic Party's leftward slide has affected the way in which it has governed American cities from coast to coast. First, he describes how the cities of yesteryear were generally run:

> "The great American cities of the early 20th century were run for the most part by politicians whose allegiance was to the New Deal, many of them autocrats who held office for decades. But they were judged on how well their policies produced real-life solutions for the poor and how well they translated the poor into the middle class. Voters and residents were interested only in one thing: whether or not the cities [that] these politicians managed, 'worked'."

But by the early 1970s, writes Collier, "the pragmatic centrists who had defined this [Democratic] Party for a generation and had built vibrant and eminently livable cities were defeated by 'New Politics' liberals who were soon calling themselves 'progressives' and who proceeded to make these cities into mad laboratories for their leftist ideological experiments."[9]

With this background in mind, let us take a close look at what has happened in so many U.S. cities where, over the past half-century, Democratic mayors and their administrations have controlled the levers of political power for years and, in many cases, decades on end.[10]

A Cautionary Tale: Detroit

To help clarify exactly how Democratic leftists have turned dozens of successful, bustling, affluent, and well-ordered American cities into dens of poverty and hotbeds of crime during the past 50 years or so, it would be instructive to briefly study one of the most egregious real-world examples—the city of Detroit, Michigan.

Though today it is the very emblem of decline and failure, Detroit was, not all that long ago, one of America's brightest success stories. In the 1920s, when the city was thriving as the home of the "Big Three" auto makers, journalist Matthew Josephson observed: "Nowhere in the world may the trend of the new industrial cycle be perceived more clearly than in Detroit. In this sense it is the most modern city in the world, the city of tomorrow."[11] More recently, historian Jeffrey Mirel put it this way: "Throughout the 1920s, Detroit was the shining star of the new era, the very center of the American economic universe, where capitalism and technology combined to produce the greatest goods for the greatest numbers."[12] The city's public schools were likewise models of excellence. In a 1924 nationwide survey of school superintendents, Detroit schools ranked higher than virtually all others in terms of their organizational efficiency and "excellence in teaching reading, writing, composition, and arithmetic."[13] Three years later, *New Republic* magazine described the Detroit Public Schools system as "one of the finest in the world."[14]

This climate of prosperity and achievement naturally attracted many newcomers to Detroit. Between 1900 and 1930, the city's population increased from 285,000 to 1.5 million.[15] And the good times were just getting started. According to one University of Michigan report: "After World War II, Detroit was leading the country's economy."[16] In his book *The Origins of the Urban Crisis: Race & Inequality in Postwar Detroit*, historian Thomas Sugrue writes that the Motor City accounted for fully "1/6 of the country's employment at mid-century."[17] By 1960, Detroit had the highest per capita income of any city in the United States.[18]

But then, things began to change for the worse. After having been governed by Republican mayoral administrations for 43 of the preceding 50 years, Detroit was permanently taken over by Democrats in 1961. In the 58 years that have passed since then, the city has not elected a single Republican mayor. Perhaps even more remarkable is the fact that only *one* Republican has served on its city council since 1970.[19] And as Detroit became a Democratic political monoculture, it became a failed city as well.

The first mayor of Detroit's Democratic Party era was Jerome Cavanagh (1962-70), a white liberal who greatly increased the city's dependence on federal financial assistance.[20] Most notably, he persuaded President Lyndon Johnson to designate a portion of Detroit as a pilot location for the so-called "Model Cities" program that Johnson launched in 1966 as part of his Great Society and War On Poverty campaigns. The advocates of this program were confident that if enough federal money were to be pumped into "affordable housing" and social welfare initiatives, even the most blighted ghettos could be rehabilitated.[21] But a few years and nearly half-a-billion federal dollars later,[22] that fantasy stood completely discredited. Because Model Cities promoted dependence on government rather than entrepreneurship and self-reliance, its "beneficiaries" gained nothing of any lasting value. By 1990, Detroit's Model City district had lost more than three-fifths of its population and nearly half of its housing units.[23]

In 1974, Democrat Coleman Young, a secret member of the Communist Party, began a 20-year stint as Detroit's first black mayor. Leftists saw him as a beacon of hope—a swaggering, charismatic man who was seemingly well-suited to help the city recapture the glories of its past. Political science professor Wilbur C. Rich, for instance, once praised Young as someone whose unflappable "confidence" and "flamboyant style" "represents the strength that many blacks believe they lack."[24]

But the real-world accomplishments of Young's mayoralty fell far short of the hype. As Manhattan Institute scholar Steven Malanga writes, Young, from an economic standpoint, "lacked a plan except to go to war with the city's major institutions and demand that the federal government save it with subsidies"—a strategy that critics referred to as "tin-cup urbanism."[25] During Young's tenure in office, Detroit's debt rating reached junk status—the lowest possible designation.[26] Moreover, the city's economy lost nearly 200,000 jobs between 1967-85, while its welfare rolls quadrupled during roughly that same period.[27]

Mayor Young also earned a reputation as someone who routinely branded white people who opposed him and his policies as "racists."[28]

Many leftists saw this contentious spirit as something positive. For instance, one fawning *Michigan Chronicle* opinion piece lauded Young as an "unapologetically black" "hero to the people of Detroit" whose "combativeness on race endeared him to blacks."[29]

Former *New York Times* public editor Daniel Okrent, by contrast, correctly portrayed Young's mayoralty as the "corrosive two-decade rule of a black politician who cared more about retribution than about resurrection."[30] Similarly, a *Washington Post* op-ed piece described Young as someone who promoted "racial divisiveness" and "did little to try and mend fences broken down along racial lines."[31]

Indeed, Young made extensive use of racially charged rhetoric. He once claimed, for instance, that whites "could not stand for black folks to control a damn thing, and if we [blacks] do, they're going to destroy it."[32] Young directed a similar brand of acrimony toward fellow blacks who opposed him, routinely smearing them as "Uncle Toms."[33] When a black councilman named Ernest Browne ran for mayor against the incumbent Young in 1977 and attracted considerable white support, Young said derisively: "We have a curious phenomenon in this campaign, perhaps an important first in American politics—a black white hope."[34]

Young's approach to crime-fighting, meanwhile, was an unmitigated failure from the outset. While acknowledging, in the earliest days of his mayoralty, that violent criminality was indeed a problem in his city, he maintained that it was "not *the* problem." Rather, said Young, "the police are the major threat" to local black people.[35] He made it clear that officers were to refrain from arresting or detaining blacks in disproportionately high numbers, regardless of how many crimes they may have committed. As a black former policeman in Detroit candidly told journalist Tamar Jacoby: "I wouldn't write tickets for black kids."[36]

Mayor Young cut the Detroit police force by 20% in 1976 as a means of addressing the city's enormous budget deficit, a move that promptly caused local crime rates to rise to unprecedented heights. By 1987, Detroit's homicide rate was three times higher than it had been two decades earlier.[37] But when residents complained about runaway crime, Young characterized their calls for "law and order" as nothing more than "code" for "Keep the ni**ers in their place."[38] His chief of police, William Hart, similarly dismissed complaints about the city's soft approach to crime as "racism and sour grapes."[39]

Young was a master of deflecting blame onto others, and doing so with a racial twist. In the fall of 1986, for example, he refused to approve a handgun ban in Detroit, on the theory that his constituents needed weapons with which to defend themselves against the "hostile white suburbs" that surrounded them.[40]

The late political scientist James Q. Wilson observed that by the end of Young's tenure as mayor, Detroit was "a fiscal and social wreck."[41] And the city's decline continued under subsequent Democratic mayors. Today, Detroit's population has a median per capita income of just $16,433 and a median household income of $27,838; both figures are about half the corresponding national medians.[42] The city's poverty rate, meanwhile, is 34.5%—about three times the overall U.S. average.[43]

None of these unhappy trends have been a result of coincidence or bad luck. Detroit's current economic malaise was brought about by decades of Democratic government policies that Hoover Institution scholar Thomas Sowell has aptly dubbed the "Detroit Pattern"—a blend of corrosive practices that include "increasing taxes, harassing businesses, and pandering to unions."[44] These three factors merit a closer look.

1) *Taxes*: From the 1960s onward, Detroit's political leaders have repeatedly imposed onerous tax increases on a base of taxpayers whose numbers have been dwindling as a result of the city's diminishing quality of life. According to a 2016 report published jointly by the Lincoln Institute of Land Policy and the Minnesota Center for Fiscal Excellence, Detroit's homeowner property taxes are the second-highest of any American city, while its commercial property taxes are the highest in the nation. These oppressive taxes continue to drive both homeowners and entrepreneurs out of Detroit and into the surrounding suburbs.[45]

2) *Harassing Businesses*: Over the past half-century, Detroit's Democratic mayoral administrations have instituted a complex web of incomprehensible governmental regulations that have choked the life out of small businesses in the city.[46] A report by Dana Berliner, Senior Vice President of the Institute For Justice, observes that many aspiring entrepreneurs in Detroit "simply give up their business dreams" because of the massive amounts of "time and money" which they must expend in order to comply with "all the regulatory requirements" of the city's "stupefying bureaucracy." "Detroiters hoping to open a business," Berliner elaborates, "face a multitude of … inspections and inspection fees, incomprehensible building requirements, expensive, mandatory public hearings, arbitrary discretion by officials, and lengthy processing delays [that] combine to discourage entrepreneurs from undertaking business ventures or improving existing ones."[47] In 2013, economist Dean Stansel conducted an "economic freedom" study that ranked the regulatory and tax climates of 384 U.S. metro areas, and found that Detroit placed a dismal 345th.[48]

3) *Pandering to Unions*: Detroit's vast bureaucracy is dominated by public-sector labor unions whose leaders and members alike have been reliable supporters of Democratic candidates during every election cycle. To reward this loyalty at the polls while simultaneously incentivizing its continuance, one Democratic political administration after another has lavished the members of these unions with high salaries, lucrative pensions, and top-of-the-line health benefit packages. These massive expenditures have placed an enormous and unsustainable financial burden on the city. For example, in 2013 the *Washington Post* reported that each month, Detroit's government was sending out more than $33 million in checks to 21,000 public-sector retirees and their families. Meanwhile, only 9,700 workers were actively employed by the city at that time.[49] Moreover, the pension obligations that Detroit owed to its retirees accounted for about half of the city's $18-to-$20 billion in long-term unfunded debt liabilities.[50]

Even as Detroit's population has declined by more than 60 percent over the past 60 years, the size of its city government has scarcely shrunk at all. In 2013, Kyle Smith reported in *Forbes* magazine:

> "All you really need to know about Detroit, which is facing a
> $327 million budget gap, is that last year it was discovered
> to still be paying for a 'horseshoer' (or farrier) on the Detroit
> Water & Sewer Department (DWSD) payroll. This individual
> costs some $56,000 in pay and benefits, despite the city not
> having any horses to shoe in his department."[51]

Because DWSD jobs are union positions, they are widely considered
sacrosanct, as evidenced by the local union president's assertion that it
was "not possible" to eliminate even the most unnecessary jobs. In
fact, writes Kyle Smith, "union bosses insisted [that] the DWSD ...
needs more, not fewer, such unionized employees," even though "an
independent report said [that] four out of five employees in the bloated
department were redundant and discovered a thicket of union
regulations driving up costs."[52]

Because of such excesses—and many others like them—by early 2013
Detroit's fiscal condition had become so dire that Michigan Governor
Rick Snyder appointed attorney Kevyn Orr to serve as the city's
emergency financial manager.[53] By Orr's telling, "years of budgetary
restrictions, mismanagement, crippling operational practices, and, in
some cases, indifference or corruption" had led to the "dysfunctional
and wasteful" condition in which Detroit now found itself.[54] Fully
one-third of the "insolvent" city's budget deficit, he said, was being
spent on retiree benefits for former public-sector employees.[55] When
Orr recommended cuts to those benefits, Detroit's two largest
municipal pension funds sued in state court to prevent such a course of
action. Thus, the city was forced to file for the largest municipal
bankruptcy in American history on July 18, 2013.[56]

Jarrett Skorup, the director of marketing and communications at the
Mackinac Center for Public Policy, explains that most of Detroit's
present-day economic woes are the ramifications of socialist policies
that have been implemented year after year by the city's Democratic
mayors and their administrations:

> "The generally accepted definition of socialism, by academics
> and the U.S. Socialist Party, is government ownership or

control of the means of production. This can be accomplished by authoritarian dictators … or it can be done democratically by a vote of elected officials. Either way, this is the defining characteristic of socialism.

"Using that definition, Detroit is more socialist than most. Michigan's largest city relies heavily on government jobs. It has the highest income and property taxes in the state and more regulations than any other city. For 60 years, the city has focused on a central planning economic model …

"It's true that Detroit was much more prosperous five or more decades ago. Its prosperity then came not from government planning, but rather the power of the free market. Ingenuity driven by competition, especially in auto making, helped make it one of the wealthiest cities on the planet. And while its decline was a complicated affair involving many factors, the expansion of government control over the economy was key."[57]

Compounding its catastrophic financial problems, Detroit has long ranked as one of the most dangerous places in the United States. The city's homicide rate is now approximately 8.5 times greater than the national average; the robbery rate is about 4.3 times the national average; the assault rate is 5.9 times the national average; and the rape rate is 2.9 times the national average.[58]

As we contemplate the facts presented in this brief thumbnail sketch of Detroit's economic and social collapse, one jarring, undeniable reality shouts out at us: This *all* happened under Democratic leadership. Indeed, a strong case could be made that Detroit, during the past five or six decades, has been one of the most purely and unanimously Democratic cities in all of American history. With that in mind, recall, for a moment, the quotes from the official Democratic Party Platform which were cited at the beginning of this pamphlet, where Democrats vowed to:

- create "an economy that … puts a middle-class life within reach for more Americans";

- "develop a national strategy ... to combat poverty" with particular "focus on ... underserved communities";
- implement "a comprehensive agenda to invest in America's cities"; and
- "support entrepreneurship and small business growth" therein.

The vast chasm between these lofty pledges on the one hand, and the reality of life in Democrat-controlled Detroit on the other, should make any self-identified Democrat think long and hard about why that chasm exists.

The Relationship Between Political Leadership and Violent Crime in America's Cities

All cities have their own unique histories, and the causes of their respective current conditions are varied and complex. But the story of Detroit is highly instructive, for it crystallizes the enormous amount of needless human suffering that can result from ill-advised public policies instituted by a political party dedicated to big government, high taxes, the strangulation of free markets, and the coddling of criminals under the banner of "social justice."

By contrast, public policies that are, for instance, tough on crime, can have a very different effect on people's quality of life in a given city. Perhaps the most remarkable example of what an enormous difference a strong approach to crime-fighting can make, is what occurred in New York City under Republican Mayor Rudolph Giuliani. During the 24-year period of Democratic governance (1969-93) that preceded his election, homicides in New York had reached historically high levels.[59] During the sole term (1989-93) of Giuliani's immediate predecessor, Mayor David Dinkins, the incidence of homicide in the city twice exceeded an unprecedented 2,000 in a single calendar year. But when Giuliani replaced Dinkins in 1993, he quickly turned things around by instituting a proactive anti-crime strategy that incorporated the use of: (a) "stop-question-and-frisk" policies;[60] (b) "CompStat" technology that allowed the Police Department to instantly identify and target criminal hot-spots with pinpoint accuracy;[61] and (c) the so-called "broken windows" philosophy of law-enforcement.

The "broken windows" theory of policing is founded on the premise that maintaining urban environments in a well-ordered condition prevents not only low-level transgressions from occurring, but also the commission of more serious crimes. Social scientists James Q. Wilson and George L. Kelling introduced the theory in a famous article titled "Broken Windows," which appeared in the March 1982 edition of *The Atlantic Monthly*. "Social psychologists and police officers tend to agree," the authors wrote, "that if a window in a building is broken and is left unrepaired, all the rest of the windows will soon be broken. This is as true in nice neighborhoods as in rundown ones. Window-breaking does not necessarily occur on a large scale because some areas are inhabited by determined window-breakers, whereas others are populated by window-lovers; rather, one unrepaired broken window is a signal that no one cares, and so breaking more windows costs nothing. (It has always been fun.)"[62]

To combat this mindset, Giuliani and his police chief, William Bratton, instructed NYPD officers to more strictly enforce existing laws against such relatively minor infractions as subway-fare evasion, public drinking, public urination, and shakedown operations by windshield-washing "squeegee men."[63] Thanks to these and other complementary law-enforcement practices, the rates of both petty and serious crimes in New York City fell suddenly and dramatically. As Manhattan Institute scholar Heather Mac Donald wrote in 2009: "It turned out that by going after low-level miscreants, you caught felons as well. A vicious murderer was arrested when he jumped a subway turnstile."[64] In a 2018 interview with Ben Weingarten, Mac Donald elaborated further on the significance of Giuliani's achievement:

> "We learned that enforcement works, that a society that sets a norm and sets consequences for its violation and enforces those consequences, can actually have an effect on human behavior. The urban violence that was taken for granted as the constitutional condition of American cities, it turns out, was the result of society simply laying down helplessly and saying,

'There's nothing we can do about crime. It's a *cri de coeur* against racism, and we just have to suck it up and accept it.' No. Enforcement works, and that is an incredibly radical and powerful message."[65]

Notably, the very antithesis of Giuliani's approach to crime was on display in two other major U.S. cities—St. Louis and Baltimore—at precisely that same time.

St. Louis elected Democrat Mayor Freeman Bosley Jr. in early 1993, and his ensuing four years in office were marked by a deep-seated reluctance to deal forcefully with his city's exploding crime problem. From the beginning of his mayoral tenure, the idealistic Bosley tried to arrange friendly meetings between himself and local gang members, urging the latter to stay in school and assuring them that "I'm committed to finding you jobs." He also told the media some details about what was said at those meetings:

> "When I talk to young people and ask why do we have so much violence, why the drive-bys, why the gangbanging? They say: 'We just don't have anything to do.' I've had young people tell me that violence is just another form of recreation."[66]

In an effort to remedy this problem, Bosley convinced a number of corporate sponsors to offer paid summer jobs to St. Louis students. He also established several community schools with recreation centers that remained open until late at night, in hopes of keeping young people occupied and out of trouble. And he persuaded city corporations to bankroll a Midnight Basketball League for similar purposes.[67] Notwithstanding all these efforts, Bosley's first year in office was the bloodiest in St. Louis history, with 267 homicides. In 1994, the death toll was only slightly less horrific: 248.[68]

In the 1990s as well, the city of Baltimore became an exceedingly dangerous place as a result of Democratic Mayor Kurt Schmoke's ineffective approach to addressing street crime and drug trafficking. By the end of the decade, the murder rate in Baltimore was six times higher than in New York City. "Under Schmoke's crime-tolerant community-policing regime," wrote Manhattan Institute Senior Fellow Fred Siegel and co-author Van Smith in the Winter 2001 edition of *City Journal*, "locals nicknamed Baltimore 'Bodymore, Murderland,' for it had become the second-deadliest city in the nation, with more than 300 murders a year, for ten years running." Approximately three-fourths of those killings were drug-related—symptoms of a brutal drug-turf war that was permitted to destroy many black neighborhoods in particular. One Baltimore police sergeant lamented that under Schmoke's ineffectual leadership, the city had fallen "in love with its own victimhood."[69]

An advisory group's 1999 report to Schmoke's successor, incoming mayor Martin O'Malley, lamented Baltimore's "rampant and unabated violent crime." Said the report:

> "For more than a decade now, the goal of efficient and effective administration of justice in Baltimore City has largely been unrealized due to neglect, indifference and political machinations.... Our Police Department has become demoralized by its inability to curb the surge of violence. Under-resourced and overwhelmed, our city's judicial branch and State's Attorney's office are ineffective in reducing the plight of crime raging in our neighborhoods."[70]

The longtime NYPD veteran Ed Norris concurred: "This culture of 'can't do' became pervasive in the [Baltimore] police department. Over the last ten years, maybe longer, they were told, as a police department: you can't do it, don't try, don't arrest drug dealers, you can only get us in trouble if you take proactive steps, you can't do anything about it unless [drugs] are legalized. Enforcement was something that was really frowned upon."[71]

The Most Dangerous Cities in America

Let us now examine which political parties are currently in charge of the most dangerous American cities with populations of 25,000 or more people. "Danger," for purposes of this analysis, is defined in terms of the number of violent crimes committed per 1,000 residents. Four categories of violent crime are included in these calculations: (a) homicide, the willful killing of one human being by another; (b) rape, which includes all forms of non-consensual sexual penetration; (c) armed robbery, defined as the actual or attempted seizure of property from a person by means of actual or threatened force; and (d) aggravated assault, which is an attack committed against a person for the purpose of inflicting severe bodily injury. The statistics regarding the incidence of each of these crimes in each city were derived from FBI records and were compiled and published in January 2019 by the custom analytics website NeighborhoodScout.com.[72]

Our list shows the 50 cities that: (a) have the highest violent crime rates in the United States; (b) are governed by mayors who are clearly identifiable as either Democrats or Republicans;[73] and (c) have either a "Mayor-Council" (MC) form of government, a "Council-Manager" (CM) form of government, or a Hybrid (HYB) of the two.[74] Of those 50 cities, 48 are currently governed by Democratic mayors and administrations; only 2 are governed by Republicans.

Rank	Cities with Populations of 25,000+	Population[75]	Type of Govt.	Violent Crimes/ 1,000	Mayor's Party
1	Bessemer, AL	26,386	MC	29.8	Democratic
2	East St. Louis, IL	26,662	CM	27.8	Democratic
3	Monroe, LA	49,761	MC	22.8	Democratic
4	St. Louis, MO	318,416	MC	20.9	Democratic
5	Detroit, MI	672,829	MC	20.6	Democratic
6	Baltimore, MD	614,664	MC	20.4	Democratic
7	Memphis, TN	652,752	MC	20.1	Democratic
8	Camden, NJ	74,417	MC	19.7	Democratic
9	Flint, MI	97,379	MC	19.7	Democratic
10	Pine Bluff, AR	42,984	MC	18.6	Democratic
11	Danville, IL	31,424	MC	17.4	Republican[76]
12	Kansas City, MO	481,360	CM	17.1	Democratic
13	Wilmington, DE	71,455	MC	17.0	Democratic
14	Little Rock, AR	198,546	CM	16.5	Democratic
15	Rockford, IL	147,404	MC	16.2	Democratic
16	Chester, PA	34,133	MC	16.1	Democratic

17	Milwaukee, WI	595,070	MC	16.1	Democratic
18	Cleveland, OH	385,810	MC	15.6	Democratic
19	Alexandria, LA	47,334	MC	14,6	Democratic
20	Stockton, CA	307,057	CM	14.3	Democratic
21	Albuquerque, NM	559,270	MC	13.9	Democratic
22	Riviera Beach, FL	34,674	MC	13.7	Democratic
23	Indianapolis, IN	852,506	MC	13.5	Democratic
24	East Point, GA	35,282	MC	13.5	Democratic
25	Oakland, CA	419,987	HYB	13.2	Democratic
26	Lake Worth, FL	38,107	CM	13.0	Republican
27	Florence, SC	37,778	CM	12.9	Democratic
28	Trenton, NJ	84,065	MC	12.8	Democratic
29	Newburgh, NY	28,363	CM	12.7	Democratic
30	Wheeling, WV	27,066	CM	12.3	Democratic
31	Charleston, WV	47,929	MC	12.3	Democratic
32	Kalamazoo, MI	75,988	CM	12.3	Democratic
33	Anchorage, AK	298,192	HYB	12.1	Democratic
34	Compton, CA	97,537	CM	12.0	Democratic
35	Jackson, MI	32,704	CM	11.8	Democratic
36	Canton, OH	71,329	MC	11.8	Democratic[77]
37	Nashville, TN	688,901	MC	11.7	Democratic
38	Harrisburg, PA	49,192	MC	11.5	Democratic
39	Albany, GA	74,904	MC	11.5	Democratic
40	Niagara Falls, NY	48,460	MC	11.4	Democratic
41	Lansing, MI	117,400	MC	11.4	Democratic[78]
42	New Orleans, LA	391,495	MC	11.4	Democratic
43	Houston, TX	2,304,388	MC	11.2	Democratic
44	Atlantic City, NJ	38,429	MC	11.0	Democratic
45	Daytona B., FL	66,649	MC	11.0	Democratic
46	Minneapolis, MN	413,645	MC	11.0	Democratic
47	Chicago, IL	2,704,965	MC	11.0	Democratic
48	Hartford, CT	123,287	MC	10.9	Democratic
49	Holyoke, MA	40,341	MC	10.9	Democratic
50	Pontiac, MI	59,792	MC	10.9	Democratic

From whichever angle we look at urban America, the stark reality of Democratic Party failure stares back at us directly. Let us consider, for example, the 20 large U.S. cities—i.e., cities with populations of 250,000 or more people—that had the highest per capita gun-homicide rates between 2010 and 2015. Each of the top 19 cities on the list was governed by a Democratic mayoral administration. Only the 20th city, Tulsa, was headed by Republicans.[79]

Rank	Cities with Populations of 250,000+	Gun-Homicide Rate Per 100,000	Mayor's Party
1	New Orleans, LA	46.9	Democratic
2	Detroit, MI	45.0	Democratic
3	St. Louis, MO	43.8	Democratic
4	Baltimore, MD	38.1	Democratic
5	Oakland, CA	23.9	Democratic
6	Kansas City, MO	21.4	Democratic
7	Cincinnati, OH	20.4	Democratic
8	Cleveland, OH	20.0	Democratic
9	Atlanta, GA	19.4	Democratic
10	Philadelphia, PA	18.7	Democratic
11	Memphis, TN	18.7	Democratic
12	Buffalo, NY	18.3	Democratic
13	Washington, D.C.	18.2	Democratic
14	Stockton, CA	17.2	Democratic
15	Miami, FL	17.0	Democratic
16	Milwaukee, WI	16.9	Democratic
17	Pittsburgh, PA	16.8	Democratic
18	Chicago, IL	16.4	Democratic
19	Indianapolis, IN	13.7	Democratic
20	Tulsa, OK	12.8	Republican

The story was much the same with regard to urban-area shootings that did not result in the death of the victims. Of the 20 large U.S. cities that had the highest per capita rates of non-fatal shootings during the five-year period of 2010 to 2015, *every single one* was governed by a Democratic mayor.[80]

Rank	Cities with Populations of 250,000+	Non-Fatal Shooting Rate Per 100,000	Mayor's Party
1	St. Louis, MO	659.7	Democratic
2	Memphis, TN	247.1	Democratic
3	Oakland, CA	232.4	Democratic
4	Detroit, MI	153.7	Democratic

5	Pittsburgh, PA	128.1	Democratic
6	Cincinnati, OH	120.3	Democratic
7	Milwaukee, WI	105.8	Democratic
8	Baltimore, MD	102.5	Democratic
9	Atlanta, GA	90.2	Democratic
10	Miami, FL	90.0	Democratic
11	Chicago, IL	88.9	Democratic
12	Kansas City, MO	87.7	Democratic
13	Philadelphia, PA	64.2	Democratic
14	New Orleans, LA	64.0	Democratic
15	Minneapolis, MN	62.2	Democratic
16	Louisville, KY	41.9	Democratic
17	Houston, TX	41.5	Democratic
18	Columbus, OH	38.6	Democratic
19	Indianapolis, IN	38.2	Democratic
20	Jacksonville, FL	36.7	Democratic

The numbers in the foregoing charts are astonishing. What they say about the Democratic Party's approach to crime, and about the party's inability to enact policies that keep crime in check, should make every individual who has ever cast a ballot for a Democratic candidate think long and hard about why he or she should ever do so again.

The Cities with the Highest Poverty Rates

Now let us turn our attention to the question of which political parties are currently in charge of the 50 American cities with the highest poverty rates in the nation, based on Census Bureau data for 2017.[81] These are cities that: (a) have populations of 60,000 or more people; (b) are governed by mayors who are clearly identifiable as either Democrats or Republicans; and (c) have either a "Mayor-Council" (MC) form of government, a "Council-Manager" (CM) form of government, or a Hybrid (HYB) of the two.[82] Of the 50 cities on our list, 46 have Democratic mayors, and 4 have Republican mayors.

Rank	Cities with Populations of 60,000+	Population[83]	Type of Govt.	Poverty Rate (%)	Mayor's Party
1	Flint, MI	97,379	MC	38.9	Democratic
2	Gary, IN	74,186	MC	36.3	Democratic
3	Camden, NJ	74,417	MC	35.7	Democratic
4	Passaic, NJ	70,646	MC	35.0	Democratic
5	Youngstown, OH	64,301	MC	34.9	Democratic
6	Detroit, MI	672,829	MC	34.5	Democratic
7	Cleveland, OH	385,810	MC	33.1	Democratic
8	College Stn., TX	112,142	CM	32.7	Republican
9	Bloomington, IN	86,654	MC	32.4	Democratic
10	Dearborn, MI	94,430	MC	32.4	Democratic
11	Rochester, NY	208,886	MC	32.3	Democratic
12	Merced, CA	82,573	CM	31.6	Republican
13	Hartford, CT	123,287	MC	31.4	Democratic
14	Wilmington, DE	71,455	MC	30.7	Democratic
15	Muncie, IN	68,707	MC	30.7	Democratic
16	Dayton, OH	140,478	CM	30.7	Democratic
17	Reading, PA	87,575	MC	30.7	Democratic
18	Trenton, NJ	84,065	MC	30.4	Democratic
19	Gainesville, FL	131,593	CM	30.3	Democratic
20	Canton, OH	71,329	MC	30.1	Democratic[84]
21	Buffalo, NY	256,908	MC	29.6	Democratic
22	Albany, GA	74,904	MC	29.3	Democratic
23	Shreveport, LA	194,472	MC	29.3	Democratic
24	Daytona Beach, FL	66,649	MC	28.2	Democratic
25	Brownsville, TX	183,829	CM	28.1	Democratic
26	Springfield, MA	154,079	MC	27.9	Democratic
27	Newark, NJ	281,770	MC	27.8	Democratic
28	Cincinnati, OH	298,802	HYB	27.7	Democratic
29	Iowa City, IA	74,384	CM	27.3	Democratic
30	Athens-Clarke,GA[85]	125,691	MC	27.2	Democratic
31	Champaign, IL	86,649	MC	27.2	Republican
32	Lorain, OH	63,736	MC	27.2	Democratic
33	Laredo, TX	257,988	CM	27.2	Democratic
34	Baton Rouge, LA	227,707	MC	27.0	Democratic
35	Allentown, PA	120,440	MC	27.0	Democratic
36	Erie, PA	98,601	MC	26.9	Democratic
37	Mission, TX	83,566	CM	26.8	Democratic
38	Lansing, MI	117,400	MC	26.3	Democratic[86]
39	New Orleans, LA	391,495	MC	26.2	Democratic
40	Paterson, NJ	147,011	MC	25.8	Democratic
41	Philadelphia, PA	1,567,872	MC	25.7	Democratic

42	Birmingham, AL	213,434	MC	25.4	Democratic
43	Lauderhill, FL	71,635	CM	25.2	Democratic
44	Kalamazoo, MI	75,988	CM	25.2	Democratic
45	Las Cruces, NM	101,760	CM	25.0	Democratic
46	Milwaukee, WI	595,070	MC	25.0	Democratic
47	Macon-Bibb, GA[87]	152,663	MC	24.9	Democratic
48	Memphis, TN	652,752	MC	24.6	Democratic
49	Evansville, IN	119,407	MC	24.5	Republican
50	Toledo, OH	278,512	MC	24.5	Democratic

It should be noted that many of the cities in the foregoing lists have been governed by Democrats not just for a short time, but for many years, or even decades, on end. To cite just a few examples: St. Louis has been led exclusively and continuously by Democrats for the past 70 years; Detroit, 58 years; Baltimore, 51 years; Kansas City, 28 years; Wilmington, 46 years; Cleveland, 30 years; Harrisburg, 37 years; Houston, 37 years; Minneapolis, 58 years; Chicago, 88 years; Buffalo, 53 years; Cincinnati, 35 years; Philadelphia, 67 years; and Newark, 66 years. Some cities on the list have not had a Republican mayor in more than a century: Milwaukee, 111 years; Atlanta, 140 years; and New Orleans, 141 years.

The Cause of Long-Term Voter Loyalty to the Democratic Party

Obviously, big-city Democratic mayoral administrations of the past half-century have failed miserably at the task of enacting public policies capable of improving the lives of their constituents. It is equally tragic that during this very same time period, Democrats have been wildly successful at: (a) expanding the size and power of the municipal bureaucracy; (b) stigmatizing the alleged "greed" and "ruthlessness" of a free-market economic system; and (c) smearing their political adversaries as unrepentant racists, sexists, misogynists, Islamophobes, xenophobes, and homophobes. These labels bring to mind the proverbial "basket" full of wretches that Hillary Clinton famously characterized as "deplorables" during her 2016 presidential run.[88]

The relentless drumbeat of this all-too-familiar Democratic message—echoed dutifully by innumerable voices in the media, in Hollywood, in academia, and even in many churches—has successfully convinced countless millions of urban dwellers that the same political party that has been destroying their cities for the past 50 years, somehow represents their last best hope for salvation. Thus do so many of these individuals routinely and robotically give Democrats their votes in political elections. For example, in the presidential races of 2008, 2012, and 2016, voters in Detroit cast, on average, 71.3% of their ballots for the Democratic candidates. The story elsewhere was much the same: 67.8% in Cleveland; 66.6% in Milwaukee; 78.5% in Oakland; 66.5% in Camden; 67.2% in Trenton; 80.1% in New Orleans; 74.9% in Chicago; 72.5% in Hartford; 76.8% in Newark; 81.8% in St. Louis; and 83.3% in Philadelphia.[89]

Why have so many people been unable to recognize the grievous harm that Democratic policies have done to them and their loved ones? Why have they been so passionately determined to defend the Democratic Party?

One particularly compelling explanation was put forth in a famous article that appeared in the *Journal of Law, Economics, & Organization*, wherein Harvard scholars Edward Glaeser and Andrei Shleifer named the so-called "Curley Effect" after its prototype, James Michael Curley, who served four (non-consecutive) terms as the Democratic mayor of Boston between 1914 and 1950. The Curley Effect, the authors explain, is a phenomenon by which a politician may "increas[e] the relative size of [his] political base through distortionary, wealth-reducing policies."[90] A *Forbes* magazine analysis of the Curley Effect puts it this way:

> "A politician or a political party can achieve long-term dominance by tipping the balance of votes in their direction through the implementation of policies that strangle and stifle economic growth. Counterintuitively, making a city poorer leads to political success for the engineers of that impoverishment."[91]

How does this happen? The Curley Effect typically occurs when Democratic political leaders adopt policies that redistribute wealth from the prosperous to the poor. This generally causes the latter to become economically dependent upon their political patrons, and thus to become a permanently pro-Democrat voting bloc. At the same time, the people whose money the government confiscates in order to fund its redistributive policies, often migrate to other cities and states. This further solidifies the political power of Curleyist practitioners by thinning out the ranks of their opponents.

In addition, Curleyists commonly try to cement popular support for their agendas by demonizing some groups of people as diabolical exploiters of the downtrodden. As Glaeser and Shleifer write: "James Michael Curley, a four-time mayor of Boston, used wasteful redistribution to his poor Irish constituents and incendiary rhetoric to encourage richer citizens to emigrate from Boston, thereby shaping the electorate in his favor. As a consequence, Boston stagnated, but Curley kept winning elections."[92]

Recall, for a moment, former mayor Coleman Young of Detroit, who not only turned racial demagoguery into an art form, but also enacted a host of policies designed to benefit his political supporters while harming his adversaries and thereby driving them out of the city. In 1982, for instance, Young tripled a commuter tax and raised residential income tax rates by half. These measures had no impact whatsoever on Young's poorer black supporters, but they exacted a high toll on more affluent whites, many of whom already had begun flocking out of the city in response to the horrific Detroit riots of 1967. Between 1970 and 1990, the share of whites in Detroit's population dwindled from about 56% to a mere 22%.[93] As a result of this trend, Young actually *strengthened* his grip on the reins of political power in Detroit and was extremely popular with the (mostly black) voters who stayed in the city. Indeed, he was reelected four times by large margins, even as Detroit descended into veritable Third World status.[94] That is precisely what the Curley Effect looks like.

The beneficiaries of Curleyist redistributionism are typically either unable or unwilling to see the connection between left-wing policies on the one hand, and a diminished quality of life on the other. Instead, they mistakenly perceive the Democratic Party to be the noble, last line of defense that stands between them and destitution. Thus, their loyalty to the Party may persist for a very long time, regardless of how bad the conditions in their city may get.

Conclusion

The facts are crystal clear, and they are stunning. For more than 50 years, the Democratic Party has fed massive amounts of rhetoric to its many reliable voting blocs in scores of U.S. cities, assuring them of its deep and abiding concern for the lives of ordinary Americans. Yet it has delivered *absolutely nothing* in terms of measurable improvements to those lives. Instead, the Party has gradually transformed itself into a political wrecking ball whose only tangible achievement in urban America has been to perpetuate obscene levels of poverty, crime, and misery. It is a shocking record of wretched failure that can be neither ignored nor wished away.

In addition, the failure of Democratic leaders in American cities has been mirrored, in many ways, by identical failures on the state and national levels. As *Investor's Business Daily* (*IBD*) reported in July 2017, a newly released study by George Mason University's Mercatus Center found that the 10 "most fiscally sound states in the nation are all low-tax, GOP strongholds, while the 10 least-solvent states are almost all high-tax and heavily Democratic." "Of the 25 most-solvent states, all but four are solidly Republican," *IBD* noted. "Of the bottom 25 states, all but five are solidly Democratic."[95]

In October 2018, the Mercatus Center published a report that ranked the fiscal stability of U.S. states over the course of a ten-year period (2006 through 2016). "Of the 10 states that show up most frequently at the bottom of the list since 2006," said an *IBD* summary of the report, "nine are solid blue [Democrat] states. Of the 10 states with consistently the best record, all but one are solidly red [Republican] states.... [S]tates in the worst fiscal shape also tend to impose the highest tax rates in the nation…. Of the 10 most fiscally sound states, all but one impose below-average tax burdens on their residents."[96]

On the national level, perhaps the most damning indictment of the policies promoted by leftist Democrats was the stratospheric rise in crime rates that began as a result of those policies in the 1960s. In his book *The Vision of the Anointed*, Dr. Thomas Sowell notes that in 1960, the nationwide murder rate, "in proportion to population, was … just under half of what it had been in 1934." But then, as the Sixties progressed, the notion that the punishment of criminals was "dehumanizing" and unnecessarily "vindictive" gained widespread acclaim, as did the idea that the proper goal of criminal justice should be to "rehabilitate" even the most hardened felons by addressing the psychological and socioeconomic "root causes" of their bad behavior. The results of this new therapeutic approach were catastrophic, as Sowell describes:

> "Crime rates skyrocketed. Murder rates suddenly shot up until the murder rate in 1974 was more than twice as high as in 1961…. Young criminals, who had been especially favored by the new solicitude, became especially violent. The arrest rate of juveniles for murder more than tripled between 1965 and 1990…."[97]

These harsh realities bring to mind what an *Investor's Business Daily* editorial stated succinctly in March 2016: "When Democrats are in control, cities tend to go soft on crime, reward cronies with public funds, establish hostile business environments, heavily tax the most productive citizens, and set up fat pensions for their union friends. Simply put, theirs is a Blue State blueprint for disaster."[98]

It is time for serious-minded and virtuous individuals who may have long supported the Democratic Party for reasons they deemed worthy and honorable, to recognize that their party has failed and betrayed them so consistently and so monstrously, that they now have a moral imperative to walk away from it.

The prospect of doing this is undoubtedly unsettling for many. It requires courage to cast away the accumulated myths and ill-advised allegiances of a lifetime. Dead belief systems are always difficult to bury, for in doing so we enter a world we do not recognize. We watch the carefully crafted towers of our understanding crash down in ruins, and we lose an integral piece of the only reality we have ever known. We fear such change. Moreover, we recoil instinctively from the distress of openly admitting—to ourselves as well as to others—that we may have spent a very long time placing our faith in people who were wholly unworthy of it. Candace Owens, the leftist-turned-conservative who recently founded the "Blexit" movement that encourages black Americans to leave the Democratic Party,[99] has eloquently articulated her own experience:

> "A huge component of what you need, to leave the left, is humility. Do you know how much humility it took for me to say, 'I was wrong about everything and I know nothing'? You've got to be a pretty humble person and have no ego, especially if you've gone so far left, that you're on Facebook and you're on Twitter de-friending your [conservative] friends, calling them all Nazis, calling them racists. How do you then say, 'Oh wait, you know what? My bad, I was wrong'? I think that's what people struggle with, is that sometimes they just stay on the left because they've gone so far into the looney-tune direction, that they're afraid to say, 'Hey, you know what? I'm sorry. I was wrong and I'm relearning this.'"[100]

It is difficult indeed, under such circumstances, to walk away from a political party that has outlived its usefulness and squandered its moral capital. But it is also a supremely noble thing to do. No one should be scorned or mocked for being brave enough to alter their worldview as a result of new information which they have acquired. Such individuals are to be honored and celebrated for their strength of character and mind. And perhaps most significantly, it is *they* who, in the not-so-distant future, may prove to be the very people whose collective awakening helps to save our precious republic from the Democratic dragon that is breathing fire at our gate.

Notes

[1] "The 2016 Democratic Platform" (Democrats.org).

[2] Ibid.

[3] Larry Elder, "John F. Kennedy: What Would He Think of His Party?" (RealClearPolitics.com, 2-16-2017); "Remarks of Senator John F. Kennedy" (JFKlibrary.org, 3-29-1957); Dr. Rich Swier, "Remembering President John F. Kennedy, NRA Lifetime Member" (November 18, 2013).

[4] Adam Hilton, "Searching for a New Politics: The New Politics Movement and the Struggle to Democratize the Democratic Party, 1968–1978" (*New Political Science*, 3-4-2016).

[5] "What George McGovern Would Do" (George McGovern For President 1972 campaign brochure).

[6] David Horowitz, "How the Democratic Party Became the Party of Appeasement" (*History News Network*, 10-14-2004).

[7] Ronald Radosh, *Divided They Fell* (The Free Press, 1996, pp. x to xiii).

[8] "Democrats' 'Sudden' Hard-Left Turn Has Been Years in the Making" (*Investor's Business Daily*, 7-18-2018).

[9] Peter Collier, Introduction to *The New Shame of the Cities*, by John Perazzo (David Horowitz Freedom Center, 2014, ISBN: 978-1-941262-07-8).

[10] It should be noted that although the role and authority of a mayor can vary significantly from city to city, a mayor's party affiliation—and, by logical extension, the political values and priorities inherent in that affiliation—typically has a major influence on how a city is governed on a day-to-day basis. A mayor's party affiliation is also ordinarily a strong reflection of the political orientation of the voters who elect not only the mayor, but often the city council members or aldermen as well. And of course, anyone appointed to a city government position by a mayor is likewise a reflection of the mayor's political philosophy. The various permutations of city governments, mayoral duties, and city council duties are explained well by Ballotpedia.org. To access that information, see https://ballotpedia.org/Mayor-council_government. Also see https://bloomp.net/articles/three-forms-of-city-government.htm.

In many of the cities that are examined in this pamphlet, the members of their city councils or boards of aldermen are openly affiliated with the Democratic Party in overwhelming numbers. For example, all 29 members of the St. Louis city council are Democrats, while Philadelphia's 16-member city council includes 13 Democrats and 3 Republicans.

Meanwhile, in many other cities, the city council members are officially listed as "nonpartisan." Frequently they are unwilling to publicly reveal what their actual party affiliations, apart from their roles as city council members, may be. But this certainly does not mean that they are apolitical. For instance, all 15 of Milwaukee's city council members are technically designated as "nonpartisan," but 5 of them are known to be longtime committed Democrats, and one (Robert Donavan) ran twice for elected office on the Republican Party ticket during the 1980s. Similarly, Detroit's 9 city council members are all identified officially as "nonpartisan," but 6 of the 9 are known to be longtime committed Democrats. (Source: "List of Current City Council Officials of the Top 100 Cities in the United States" (Ballotpedia.org, information accessed April 1, 2019).

[11] Jeffrey Mirel, *The Rise and Fall of an Urban School System: Detroit, 1907-81* (University of Michigan Press, Second Edition, 1999, Chapter 2).

[12] Ibid.

[13] *The Detroit Educational Bulletin*, Vol. 9, January 1924, p. 4.

[14] Jeffrey Mirel, "Urban Public Schools in the Twentieth Century: The View from Detroit" (Cited in *Brookings Papers on Education Policy, 1999* (Edited by Diane Ravitch, p. 18).

[15] Pamela Engel, "These Photos of Detroit's Golden Age Show How Far the City Has Fallen" (*Business Insider*, 7-20-2013).

[16] "A Brief 20th Century History of Detroit" (University of Michigan).

[17] Ibid.

[18] Kevin D. Williamson, "Detroit Goes Down" (*National Review*, 7-19-2013).

[19] "America Is Driving Down the Same Road That Bankrupted Detroit" (*Washington Examiner*, 7-28-2013).

[20] "Detroit's Socialist Nightmare Is America's Future" (DailyReckoning.com).

[21] *The Model Cities Program* (Dept. of Housing & Urban Development, 1971; "The Muddled Model Cities Model" (*New York Times*, 7-3-1992).

[22] Steven Koven and Andrea Koven, *Growth, Decline, and Regeneration in Large Cities: A Case Study Approach* (Routledge Publishing, 2018).

[23] W. Dennis Keating and Norman Krumholz, *Rebuilding Urban Neighborhoods: Achievements, Opportunities, and Limits* (Sage Publications, 1999, p. 111).

[24] Wilbur C. Rich, *Coleman Young and Detroit Politics* (Wayne State University Press, 1989, p. 34).

[25] Elise Hilton, "The Death of Detroit's Middle Class" (Acton Institute, 7-29-2013); Steven Malanga, "We Don't Need Another War on Poverty" (*City Journal*, Autumn 2008).

[26] Jena McGregor, "What Killed Detroit? Let's Not Forget the Who" (*Washington Post*, 7-29-2013).

[27] David Schaafsma, *Eating on the Street: Teaching Literacy in a Multicultural Society* (University of Pittsburgh Press, 1993, p. 75).

[28] "Detroit After Coleman Young" (*The Blade*, 6-26-1993).

[29] Brandon Hunter, "Coleman Young: A History of the People's Mayor" (*Michigan Chronicle*, 5-24-2018).

[30] W. Kim Heron, "Time's Warp – and the Legacy of Coleman Young" (*Detroit*

Metro Times, 10-1-2009).

[31] McGregor, op. cit.

[32] Robert J. Norrell, *The House I Live In: Race In The American Century* (Oxford University Press, 2003, p. 273).

[33] Hunter, op. cit.

[34] "Coleman Young: The 10 Greatest Myths" (*Detroit Free Press*, 5-26-2018).

[35] Norrell, op. cit., p. 273.

[36] Steven Malanga, "The Next Wave of Urban Reform" (*City Journal*, Autumn 2010).

[37] Schaafsma, op. cit., p. 75.

[38] Norrell, op. cit., p. 273.

[39] Steven Malanga, "The Next Wave of Urban Reform" (*City Journal*, Autumn 2010).

[40] Stephen Franklin, "Murders Torment Detroit" (*Chicago Tribune*, 1-13-1987).

[41] James Q. Wilson, "The Closing of the American City" (*The New Republic*, 5-11-1998).

[42] Quickfacts: Detroit and The United States (U.S. Census Bureau).

[43] Quickfacts: United States (U.S. Census Bureau).

[44] Thomas Sowell, "Obama Administration Is Following the 'Detroit Pattern'" (TownHall.com, 3-22-2011).

[45] Lincoln Institute of Land Policy and Minnesota Center for Fiscal Excellence, "50-State Property Tax Comparison Study" (June 2016); "Detroit Has the Second-Highest Residential Property Taxes in the Nation, Says Study" (*Daily Detroit*, 6-16-2016).

[46] Scott Beyer, "Root Causes of Detroit's Decline Should Not Be Ignored" (NewGeography.com, 8-27-2013).

[47] Dana Berliner, "How Detroit Drives out Motor City Entrepreneurs" (Scribd.com).

[48] Dean B. Stansel, "An Economic Freedom Index for U.S. Metropolitan Areas" (*The Journal of Regional Analysis & Policy*, 2013).

[49] Brad Plumer, "Detroit's Pension Problems, in One Chart" (*Washington Post*, 7-19-2013); John Reeves, "19 Shocking Facts about Detroit's Bankruptcy," *USA Today*, 12-3-2013).

[50] Rich Tucker, "Detroit and the Bankruptcy of Liberalism" (*Daily Signal*, 7-22-2013; John Reeves, "19 Shocking Facts about Detroit's Bankruptcy," *USA Today*, 12-3-2013).

[51] Kyle Smith, "Detroit Gave Unions Keys to the City, and Now Nothing Is Left" (*Forbes*, 2-21-2013); Jarrett Skorup, "No Horses, but Detroit Water Department Employs 'Horseshoer'," 8-20-2012).

[52] Ibid.

[53] Monica Davey, "Michigan Naming Fiscal Manager to Help Detroit" (*New York Times*, 3-1-2013).

[54] Associated Press, "Report by Emergency Manager Says Detroit's Finances Are Crumbling, Future Is Bleak" (Fox News, 5-13-2013).

[55] Ibid; "Detroit Clearly 'Insolvent,' Says Emergency Manager" (BBC, 5-13-2013);

Matt Helms and Joe Guillen, "Financial Manager: Detroit 'Dysfunctional,' Wasteful" (*USA Today*, 5-13-2013).

[56] "Detroit Files for Bankruptcy Protection" (*USA Today*, 7-18-2013).

[57] Jarrett Skorup, "Socialism Didn't Make Detroit Great" (Mackinac Center for Public Policy, 9-5-2018).

[58] "Crime Rate in Detroit, Michigan" (City-data.com).

[59] "New York City Population and Number of Homicides by Year" (Reddit.com).

[60] Heather Mac Donald, "Don't Take the Wrong Lessons from New York City's Murder Drop" (*National Review Online*, 12-28-2017).

[61] "Compstat Policing: Definition, Process, and Model" (Study.com, Chapter 6, Lesson 21).

[62] George L. Kelling and James Q. Wilson, "Broken Windows" (*The Atlantic*, March 1982).

[63] Elaine Woo, "James Q. Wilson Dies at 80; Pioneer in 'Broken Windows' Approach to Improve Policing" (*Los Angeles Times*, 3-3-2012).

[64] Heather Mac Donald, "Safe Cities, Successful Conservatives" (*The Guardian*, 2-24-2009).

[65] Ben Weingarten, "Heather Mac Donald on Corrosive Identity Politics, Multiculturalism and Unjust Criminal Justice" (6-6-2018).

[66] Laurel S. Walters, "Mayor Finds Bully Pulpit, Few Resources in St. Louis" (*Christian Science Monitor*, 4-18-1994).

[67] Ibid.

[68] Doyle Murphy, "2015 Was St. Louis' Deadliest Year in Two Decades" (*Riverfront Times*, 1-1-2016).

[69] Fred Siegel and Van Smith, "Can Mayor O'Malley Save Ailing Baltimore?" (*City Journal*, Winter 2001).

[70] Peter Hermann and Ivan Penn, "Justice Report Urged in City..." (*Baltimore Sun*, 12-17-1999).

[71] Siegel and Smith, op. cit.

[72] Dr. Andrew Schiller, "NeighborhoodScout's Most Dangerous Cities – 2019" (NeighborhoodScout.com, 2-2-2019); "How We Rank the 100 Most Dangerous Cities List" (NeighborhoodScout.com, 2-2-2019).

[73] Any cities on NeighborhoodScout's "Most Dangerous" list that are currently led by mayors who identify politically as "Independent," "Nonpartisan," "Bipartisan," or "Other"—rather than as either "Democratic" or "Republican"—are not included on our list. Thus, the 50th-ranked city on our list, Pontiac (Michigan), is actually #60 on the NeighborhoodScout list, meaning that 10 of the top 60 cities on the NeighborhoodScout list have been excluded from our list because they are not led politically by either a Democratic or Republican mayor. The 10 excluded cities are: Gadsden, AL; Saginaw, MI; Myrtle Beach, SC; San Bernardino, CA; Springfield, MO; Texarcana, TX; Shawnee, OK; Muskogee, OK; Clinton, IA; and Farmington, NM.

[74] As Ballotpedia.org explains, "Mayor-Council" governments can be either "Strong Mayor-Council," where the mayor is the chief executive with expansive powers, or

"Weak Mayor-Council," where the executive authority of the mayor is less expansive. Conversely, in a "Council-Manager" form of government the mayor is a regular voting member of the city council, which in turn appoints a city manager to oversee day-to-day municipal operations, draft a budget, and implement the council's policies. Still, the mayor in such a system is a major player, responsible for such tasks as presiding at council meetings, serving as a spokesperson for the community, helping elected and appointed officials work together cohesively, and assisting the council in setting goals and making policy. (See also: https://government.georgetown.org/city-management/council-manager-form-of-government/.)

[75] Population statistics for each city are derived from City-data.com and the U.S. Census Bureau.

[76] The longtime Republican mayor of Danville, Scott Eisenhauer, whose term was scheduled to run through May 7, 2019, left his post in order to take another job in October 2018 and was replaced by an Independent, Ricky Williams Jr., who would serve out the seven remaining months. For purposes of the integrity of our list, it makes the most sense, under these circumstances, to classify Danville as a Republican-led city.

[77] Though Thomas Bernabei was elected mayor of Canton in 2015 by running as a nonpartisan, he has been a lifelong Democrat. Thus, he is counted here as a Democrat.

[78] Though Lansing's city races are officially considered nonpartisan, Mayor Andy Schor is a career Democrat. Thus, he is counted here as a Democrat. See Sarah Lehr, "What Can Lansing Expect from Mayor Andy Schor?" (*Lansing Journal*, 12-29-2017).

[79] Rich Logis, "Is it Time for Martial Law in Democrat-Run Cities?" (*WorldNet Daily*, 5-17-2018); Francesca Mirabile, "Chicago Isn't Even Close to Being the Gun Violence Capital of the United States" (*The Trace*, 10-21-2016).

[80] Ibid.

[81] Any cities or localities on the Census Bureau list that are led by mayors who identify politically as "Independent," "Nonpartisan," Bipartisan," or "Other," are not included on our list. Thus, the 50th-ranked city on our list, Toledo (Ohio), is actually #59 on the Census Bureau list, meaning that 9 of the top 59 cities on the Census Bureau list have been excluded from our list because they are not led politically by either a Democratic or Republican mayor. Those 9 cities are: Syracuse, NY; Madera, CA; Greenville, NC; Davis, CA; Harlingen, TX; Pharr, TX; Florence-Graham, CA; Ames, IA; and Pine Hills, FL.

[82] As Ballotpedia.org explains, "Mayor-Council" governments can be either "Strong Mayor-Council," where the mayor is the chief executive with expansive powers, or "Weak Mayor-Council," where the executive authority of the mayor is less expansive. Conversely, in a "Council-Manager" form of government the mayor is a regular voting member of the city council, which in turn appoints a city manager to oversee day-to-day municipal operations, draft a budget, and implement the council's policies. Still, the mayor in such a system is a major player, responsible for such

tasks as presiding at council meetings, serving as a spokesperson for the community, helping elected and appointed officials work together cohesively, and assisting the council in setting goals and making policy. (See also: https://government.georgetown.org/city-management/council-manager-form-of-government/.)

[83] Population statistics for each city are derived from City-data.com and the U.S. Census Bureau.

[84] Though Thomas Bernabei was elected mayor of Canton in 2015 by running as a nonpartisan, he has been a lifelong Democrat. Thus, he is counted here as a Democrat.

[85] Athens-Clarke is a consolidated city-county located in northeastern Georgia

[86] Though Lansing's city races are officially considered nonpartisan, Mayor Andy Schor is a career Democrat. Thus, he is counted here as a Democrat. See Sarah Lehr, "What Can Lansing Expect from Mayor Andy Schor?" (*Lansing Journal*, 12-29-2017).

[87] Macon-Bibb is a consolidated city-county located in central Georgia.

[88] Katie Reilly, "Read Hillary Clinton's 'Basket of Deplorables' Remarks about Donald Trump Supporters" (*Time*, 9-10-2016).

[89] See City-data.org.

[90] Edward Glaeser and Andrei Shleifer, "The Curley Effect: The Economics of Shaping the Electorate" (*Journal of Law, Economics, & Organization*, 2005); Mark Hendrickson, "President Obama's Wealth-Destroying Goal" (*Forbes*, 5-31-2012).

[91] Hendrickson, op. cit.

[92] Glaeser and Shleifer, op. cit., p.1.

[93] "Michigan: Race and Hispanic Origin for Selected Large Cities and Other Places: Earliest Census to 1990" (Census.gov).

[94] Glaeser and Shleifer, op. cit.; Robert J. Norrell, *The House I Live In: Race In The American Century* (Oxford University Press, 2003, p. 273).

[95] John Merline, "Best-Run States Are Low-Tax Republican, Worst-Run Are High-Tax Democratic, Study Finds" (*Investor's Business Daily*, 7-11-2017).

[96] "What Do the Worst-Run States Have in Common? They're Run by Tax-and-Spend Democrats" (*Investor's Business Daily*, 10-9-2018); Eileen Norcross and Olivia Gonzalez, "Ranking the States by Fiscal Condition" (Mercatus Center at George Mason University, October 2018).

[97] Thomas Sowell, *The Vision of the Anointed* (Basic Books, 1995, pp. 21-27).

[98] "How Decades of Democratic Rule Have Ruined Some of Our Finest Cities" (*Investor's Business Daily*, 3-9-2016).

[99] Blexit—meaning "Black exit"—is a movement that encourages African Americans to leave the Democratic Party. (See "What Is Blexit?" by Fox News, 10-29-2018). Turning Point USA is a nonprofit organization whose mission is to "promote the principles of freedom, free markets, and limited government." (See www.tpusa.com/aboutus/.)

[100] "The Candace Owens Show," with guest Patrick Dennard (3-17-2019).

About the Author

John Perazzo is the managing editor of *DiscoverTheNetworks.org*, an encyclopedic guide to the political Left and a project of the David Horowitz Freedom Center. He is also a contributing writer to *Front Page Magazine*. He is the author of the book *The Myths That Divide Us: How Lies Have Poisoned American Race Relations*. He has authored such pamphlets as *Obama's War on the Young* (2013), *The New Shame of the Cities* (2014), and *The Shame of the Schools* (2018). And he has co-authored several pamphlets with David Horowitz, including: *From Shadow Party to Shadow Government: George Soros and the Effort to Radically Change America* (2011); *Occupy Wall Street: The Communist Movement Reborn* (2012); and *Government Versus the People* (2012).

www.ingramcontent.com/pod-product-compliance
Lightning Source LLC
Chambersburg PA
CBHW061232280526
45784CB00006B/2730